If momentum, as Terry Hermsen writes in his new book, is "a matter of degree," then what he measures with an exacting eye is the direction, quality, and meaning of the motion of moving bodies, his own and others, in their daily course around the sun. *A House for Last Year's Summer* shows his uncanny ability to discern eternal verities in the quotidian, and his mastery of colloquial speech makes each line ring with authenticity. In riddles and prose poems, homages to artists and places here and abroad, elegies and interludes, the poet finds a local habitation for what propels him through the world: love. This is a lovely book.
~Christopher Merrill, author of *Self-Portrait with Dogwood*

Other Books by Terry Hermsen

36 Spokes: The Bicycle Poems (Bottom Dog Press, 1985)
Child Aloft in Ohio Theatre (in *Men and Women/Women and Men*, Bottom Dog Press, 1995)
Teaching Writing from a Writer's Point of View (co-edited with Bob Fox, NCTE, 1998)
O Taste and See: Food Poems (co-edited with David Garrison, Bottom Dog Press, 2003)
The River's Daughter (Bottom Dog Press, 2009)
Poetry of Place: Helping Students Write Their Worlds (NCTE, 2009)
The Most Beautiful Cemetery in Chile (poetry by Christian Formoso, co-translated with Sydney Tammarine, Green Fish Press, 2016)

Bottom Dog Press

A House for Last Year's Summer

Poems

Terry Hermsen

Harmony Series
Bottom Dog Press
Huron, Ohio

© 2017 Terry Hermsen
& Bottom Dog Press, Inc.
ISBN   978-1-947504-01-1

Bottom Dog Press, Inc.
PO Box 425, Huron, OH 44839
Lsmithdog@aol.com
http://smithdocs.net

Credits:
General Editor and Layout Design: Larry Smith
Cover Design: Susanna Sharp-Schwacke
Copy Editor: Flora Church
Author Photo: William Walker

Acknowledgments

Gratitude to the following journals and anthologies where some of these poems have appeared: *The Ides of March* (anthology); *Fourth River Review; Lake Effect; The Louisville Review; Measure; A Rustling and Waking Within* (anthology)

CONTENTS

    1.   Lessons in Profusion

Single Oar	11
Envoi for Nate	13
Swans on Berlin Station	15
Schoolhouse on Liberty Road	16
A Dormant Order (Riddle)	17
Nap on the Furnace Run	18
Lessons in Profusion: A Sequence	19
Seven Earth Moments	20
Toward Gluck's *Orpheus*	22
For My Sister	23
Temporary Circumference (Riddle)	24
Black Cherry Trees Ripened Off of Stevenson Road	25
Groundhog Day	26
The Green Man	27

    2.   Interlude: Nine Innings   31

    3.   Spiral Jetty

Snail Along the Allegheny Trail	39
"Where Does the Dark Go When the Dark Goes Down?"	40
Self-Portrait With Drowning	41
Within One Burning Star	42
For Zita	43
Variations	44
For C.Y. Woo	45
The Peaches are Rotting in My Neighbor's Yard	46
She Lives Above the Bakery	47
RiddleWish	48
The Floating World	49
Spiral Jetty/Mirror-Span: Homage to Robert Smithson	51
Lament for the Dead from an Island in the Rain	54
On the Gift of Three Artificial Candles	55
Wrinkle in the Carpet	56
Noël Escapes	57
When the Musician Moves into His House	58
Goldfinches with Meadow	59

    4.   Interlude: Las Botellas de la Eternidad   63

5. The Smallest Ripple

Palabras Parejas	73
Age Warps	74
Fractal Walk	75
Judge and Defend (Riddle)	77
Sugar Maple	78
The Smallest Ripple	80
New Washington: A Memory	81
Mark Rothko, "Red Maroons" (1962)	82
Sonnets for a Deaf Son	83
My Father's Houses	84
The Laboratory of Return (Riddle)	85
Silence of Your Eyes	86
Beautiful Rain	87
The Elemental	88
In Africa, Ohio	89
Re-Entering Picasso's "Las Saltimbanques"	90
A Farewell for Neruda	91
A House for Last Year's Summer	93

6. Epilogue: Five Days at the End of the World

The Portal	97
Hours of Exile	98
On the Day of the Dead	99
In the Land of Fire	100
At the End of the World	101
Author Biographical Sketch	105

NOTES:
Ø   On the riddles:
Clues and answers are listed at the end of the manuscript.
Additionally, the poem following each riddle might help provide some context, as each of those poems is tangentially related to the riddle that comes before.
Ø   Any words in Spanish are italicized, with their English equivalents supplied at the end of each poem.

for my father

"*You cannot build a house
for last year's summer.*"
~African proverb

1. Lessons in Profusion

*"God! childhood!
how soon I forgot it!"*
~Kenneth O. Hanson, "The Divide"

Single Oar

The swamp so thick with muck at the southeast corner of our land
was the reason we bought that house.
Neighbors—the ones who'd become our neighbors—
told us it was peat—that offers had been made

to carve it up for sale. We, city-slickers (at least in their eyes)
fell for it, put the money down. That October
the agent met us there to bring us the keys
was darkened with clouds. Wind crept through the cracks

like knives slicing open letters. What did that house
have to tell us, its edges so threatened with overgrown lavender?
How little we knew. I'd heft wood up the hill, half-dead
trees stripped of their bark as tan and bare

as bodies in some magazine, trim them
into hunks to feed into the fire. Apples
rocked in their hordes within the cellar—
their cordoned cradle where the mice

rounded out their nests. A child (ours) hauled
her tiny violin to play on the cracked steps
that once led to a kitchen garden,
named every spot around that house

after a different tune. Fires I'd light
out on the hillside—leaves from the hovering oaks,
thistles yanked from the blackberry's caves—
I'd feel like some pioneer stranded on the prairie

and more alone. I took to brushing my face
against a passing bough of pine,
trying to conjure the feeling
of courting the sky. And once

retrieved an oar—a single oar—
from out of the muddy, reed-packed soil.
What boat had tried to cross these plains?
What man, lonely as me, left it there,

unable to row on? It stands now
in the corner of my bedroom.
Thirty years have passed like a shadow
brushing a hand over someone asleep,

leaving a song, something I might have sung,
or did, to a child awakened in the middle
of the night. That same child (grown now)
who yesterday asked me for the words.

Envoi for Nate

Lying in the creek, the stones form a pillow
waiting for the melt-off of winter deluge
or else another century of snow. They blend

the reds with starker whites and scattered browns
as if here began the range of choirs for the earth.
This stream called Furnace Run, no doubt

because the fires made its bed. Lie back, child,
it may be twenty years since I was here
but the hawk still floats above you

training his vision on your closing eyes,
as you drift in and out of a book.
Three times he passes overhead

and strikes a warning call till you are sure
it is for you alone. Maybe everything around
is yours, as the poet suggested. The stones

breathe, they carry your history, and you
are but one beckoned wave among so many
crossing each other from multiple

circumferences. Sleep then, the thefts
of the forest will replace themselves, myriads
of seeds to form one canopy,

fungi beneath the skin of the horizontal, the maples'
off-spring rising stronger below the beeches' alternate shade.
You've read that. Soon you'll rise

into these shadows, your own name
an alternate formality, stitched or striped
with the daily shift of rushes, the reddening thickets

from what will feed the closing of this sky.
I am not here—and yet the voice of the hawk
is mine, suddenly arrived in the cordoned woods

where everything that matters is invisible
or hidden behind a scalloped black trunk
as in the golden cities of the mushroom

and here before you, some small gray weight
bobbing on the balded fallen branch—these wings
that leap, flash tail-red and settle, just beyond your sight.

— A House for Last Year's Summer

Swans on Berlin Station

Momentum's such a matter of degree. Take this boy
who at four and a half already thinks too much
and cannot keep his bike in motion, stops mid-
sidewalk to discuss the word. The mole, fur

grown over her tiny eyes, digs with five-digit, wide,
incongruous paws, tunnels through the ground
at the speed of twelve feet an hour. The conductor,
grown white and bristled, gathers up the week

for his choir, strings and pushes the air through
his hands, now arched with the right to bring it close
to an imagined diaphragm, simultaneously pinched
with the left and parsed like a single note

threaded through the cloth of their darkened voices.
Then these swans on Berlin Station, farm road
toward the reservoir strung out to the east, rise from
the ditch to stop me as I barrel along at 60, the mother

and three cygnets meeting the father at the yellow stripe.
How awkward they all seem, parents rocking their unlikely
frames, feathers poured over them like aging cream,
their gray fledglings lined up for the long trek

back to water, steady, with no wings yet, no cover,
no bright and depthless surface upon which to glide.

The Schoolhouse on Liberty Road

Summer slid through the wide sills
Of that house, its thickened hours
Tethered to the rising corn. I was alone,
Each silent evening filling the high round window,
Shadows of cars circling to the loft. The old school
Turned sanctuary at the corner of the fields

Drew the ghosts of children across those fields
Wending plowed years to cross the sill
Of shifting winds. As if the school
Were a schooner—white curtains, white sails—for hours
I'd ride, pages shifting in the wide windows'
Breath as if at sea. It was all so alone—

Lilies sticky with color, hammock in lone
Circuit between two oaks. Across grim fields,
Trains rattled their coal-dark, shiny windows.
Low tracks of clouds like sculpted sills
Carried the long and stagnant hours
In tumbling herds past the lonely school.

Slowly old presences reclaimed the school
In slates like cloudy pools, recitations intoned,
Shape singing, so easily entering the echoing hours,
Measured weights, ordered feasts of field
And scale, sonnet and beaker, the sills
Of burst hearts within those windows.

I'd watch their soundless kisses from the windows,
How they'd turn, disappear inside the willow, re-schooling
Their trim hearts. Evenings I'd round the sills—
One of the olden young at last, and never lonely.
I invented souls, to punctuate the fields.
Invited winds to shake the quiet hours

From their ancient, solitary rules, the gilded hours
Of chance and choice, slim matrix of the windows.
Invented them—on days as ribbed as fields,
Regal as the robes of summer, schooled
To this borrowed shore of cloud-lonely
Sky. I'd walk out, sit upon the dusted sill,

My lone face trimmed and speckled with the hours,
A visitor still, but calm inside the windows, the school
Children heading out across the fields of age.

A Dormant Order
(a riddle)

And so you find that waves have been caught up
    in clouds of some strange
flattened sky, although no General Moon rides down
    to comb out every strand
and pull back for another surge
    at Fortress Sand. No, these knots
      are far too human: where one laps up
against your eye, another fails
    to reach your thigh, on this your
shore where you are vulnerable to tides
    within, without. So slide away, the Day
unfolds its plans—and they include you tugging at
the Gordian storm you've made
    of all your sweet beliefs
and hours, where loves long gone revive
    and houses bleed to alleyways and bowers: all
must begin again, sorted to thin dynasties,
    snapped back to continents that can pretend
      an ordered main. Your hands
are geiger counters or sliding brides—where they curl in
to wring some non-existent wish of all its worth.

    They scour now and turn
what once was sea to field: no fencerows, no errant oaks,
    no unplowed streams diagonalled across
this temporary scheme. What's left? You have
    rewrapped the presence
      of your dear travail and placed
a breasted bow atop what surely will come undone
    at any planetary turn, when you return
      and let these wide and lovely vestiged arms
        have at you again.

Terry Hermsen —

Nap on the Furnace Run

Clouds drift out of
the sycamores
some ghostly thin

like two fading lungs
side by side
and then a tangle

of bundled light
puddled up
in spots so bright

there is some kind
of snowbound bear
dancing there

and gone as the blue
got tired of itself
wanted to be

bulbous hungry
parrot wave leaping
on the back

of that same
sad long-necked
man from

minutes ago
his feet now
stretched out

on the loosened harp
of these high and lazy
earthly winds.

Lessons in Profusion: A Sequence

1

Motors in the dice. One sliver of the globe
discovers glass. And from
glass: the telescope.

2

Great-horned owls breed in crows'
or hawks' nests, harmonize
their calls in thirds. Lay eggs
in the coldest months.

3

We sit on a boulder rising from the current, and he tosses
leaves from his two-year-old hands. Odd how their reflections
on the streambed below distort to the geometric.

4

No longer does the Land of the Free
believe in its own democracy. Instead the Legislators of Fear
shape districts to make themselves perpetual.

5

Why does the rich man
beside me at the intersection, momentarily frozen
into his only shadow, mouth-sync
such an angry song?

6

Note for a fortune cookie:
Keep at least a few dead branches.

7

Patricia tells me that when she was three
on the prairies of Manitoba
she placed *"these white little round things"* into a jar
and watched them explode over days into hundreds of spiders.

Terry Hermsen —

Seven Earth Moments

Shoes off in the stream—
by the swing of her arms

she slips away from me, threatens
to return to the fish.

*

Words like stepping stones.
Some rock to one side, require

leaps, some take on the mask
of the river. Today I sit in the middle

of a swift Western stream, till it feels like me alone
that is moving. I am sixteen, have wandered off

through the woods. My parents
no longer exist.

*

Strained knee. Tendons throb.
In the bowl of the valley

I lie all evening—incredulous—
absorbing the ancient healing drums.

*

Halfway, Oregon (half-way to what?)—
on bikes we coast

ten miles down, surrounded by mountains
and yellow fields of wheat.

Every road, all over again,
teaches you how to ride.

*

Here is a storm, ripping the tarp (the heart)
away. Ivy Lea (western New York) racked

by mile-high winds off the lake. Like giants wailing.
All nouns now are capitalized. Skin.

— *A House for Last Year's Summer*

Shivering. Breaking the Lock on a vacant
Cabin. Bodies on a bare Mattress.
Waking to bright, restored, cold Sun.

    *

Edge of the lumbered
Appalachians (where thousands come

on Sundays as if in a revolving
sleep) in rainless wind

we hear it falling
our way.

    *

In Glen Helen—five thousand acres
donated to the town in his daughter's name—

we come, running away
from another meeting.

At the base of a tree you tell me how,
back in Oregon, your friend threatened

to chop down your favorite if you
followed through with your (self-)deadly plan.

Then you kissed me, in more
than a sisterly way, so that walking home

we nearly forgot to look up
to thousands of fireflies blinking

to the heights of the forest.

Toward Gluck's *Orpheus*

        for Shinichi Susuki and his Talent Education Program

Brick house at the fielded edge of Bucyrus
where Mary Ann taught music in her large red living room
while idle parents waited in the kitchen and gabbed as we would
at our offspring's awkward baseball games. What
did we know of etudes and allegro, Gluck's *Orpheus*
slowly emerging from the chrysalis of *Twinkle Little Star*?
We were to play endless cassette tapes in the car
so the tunes would thread through our five-year-olds' heads
and their fingers remember to find arched positions
on the green, red, white and yellow stripes
like runners jostling into place, to be held
a pause longer, or flicker at last to vibrato, like a shifting glance,
and shake till the air in the room lightened.

How silly we must have seemed: grownup Americans
with our wide stances following the mantra of a frail Japanese man
who after the lost war built a new empire to teach our children
European songs. We carried the tiny black cases, lunch boxes,
as if we were porters to little kings and queens. And our faces
so intense. Our discipline so harsh. All because we had
no music of our own, could not even stumblingly read
a line of those notes. But the years know how
to accumulate, enjamb, find shape, and all those bodies
grow. The music threads off. The corn from all those fields
we drove through to arrive at that red brick house
pours season after season into elevators of the dark
in golden streams. That rise again with their green shimmer.

For My Sister

Here the wrens sweep their little homes
with brooms of sound and dive through

the darkened doors, feed their brood—coded
inside, alive or not—the grubs of silence.

What else? Artists make talismans from match boxes,
little charms that slide out where cigarettes once pooled smoke,

leaves compose their endless quizzes, roots awake,
the peonies our grandma planted still nod over our heads

and you, dead now nearly a year, have not yet found your grave.
———
Sing to me, equal to equal, whether you choose shadow or pine.
———
I will begin with the hollow numbers that the night
slides under my eyes. How I hate all the edgers

and shirring blades my neighbors use to sever back
anything that grows out of line. Right now, in fact—

any hour of the summer—off in the distance, one of the soldiers
of death is burrowing away at the morning. As am I.
———
Those summers we slept so late, spooned the little nuggets
in their jostling zeroes, grew hazy before the screen, laid out

the tunneled passages where our names were changed
into the three roped mysteries of criminal intent.

Oh how well we hid behind our charts, traded inquiries
for a column of crosses, sang only the approved tunes,

had hardly stretched when the day was already over. They hid
us away, I think, Nancy, didn't want us to know

the map of our own souls. And they were right. The lakes were all
below the picnics of golden moorings. When we stepped out

who would have seen us stretch our wings?

Temporary Circumference
(a riddle)

This too large a mirror to step into,
holding onto one question
and reaching through to the other

as if the alternate sides
of your intention hung suspended
along a central, wavery plane.

There is a moment when you know: the fiery ring
of time and the tiny mouths of sound
must move as one. Now you are above,

your left foot deliberately breaking through the ice,
the other having no effective choice
except to rhyme and keep

the awkward wish to land at bay. It is
not water, though, that rises from below
but air, as from an organ shaft

which you keep playing
as the earth unfolds, what is before
and what churns after

running through you, the reel
that threads the impossible to what
is forgotten only for so long.

— A House for Last Year's Summer

Black Cherry Trees Ripened Off of Stevenson Road

for Leslie

There were butterflies, hundreds of them,
along the path to the cemetery,

though at first I thought *grasshoppers*,
they spread so thickly under our feet

and fluttered away from the source
of their heaven: those berries spilling

from the 40-foot-high fencerow, the single seeds
cased in viscous red syrup, bitter to my tongue

but enough to draw these fritillaries back up to the heights
like a melody now caught in its upper octaves.

We wheeled our bikes through
like a small caravan, our lunch packed inside

and a blanket for sleeping
all afternoon among the graves

in this August oasis
of fenced-in reverence,

its long lane a doorway
of drunken blue wings.

Terry Hermsen —

Groundhog Day
Andrew Wyeth (Philadelphia Museum of Art)

In the wrinkled valleys of Pennsylvania
Wyeth studies a single house, casts the first snow

against its huge white wall, makes study after study
of two milk cans in the cooling shed,

disappears his neighbor from her awkward pose,
then the snarl of the dog's face as well.

Paints window after window till the window's solitude
comes through, only a knife beside a white plate,

an empty cup, a moment in the pause
when the first light across the winter-browned yard

reveals each long stroke, stark tree, a jagged log
and the wrapped chain that hauled it here.

The Green Man   *(a circular/reversible poem)*

Wandering the third floor shelves : *The Green Man* —
with headshots some scholar-photographer tracked one summer
     in a grant across the gray cathedrals. Within the schema
of the great grand buttresses, admittedly a minor motif writ large
through her season's camera: dry mask within a cornice—all that weight
          above—spews oak leaves out of his eyes, or grows the forest
     like some swollen proclamation from his beard, sprouts
          the thick of a vine from a furrowed forehead, stalk
     burst through the skin. The 14th-century's fear of earthly bondage—
distant memory where our faces—or our gods—grew in the leaves.
Bacchus or the Lionhearted, or some wayward apostles'
     severed heads bowed home again—as if the forest itself
          were a chorus and thrust these stone or wooden eyes
     into arching, antiphonal hymns. As the many angels with their scales
               for weighing our grief. From drunken longings,
                    layered faces, skulls of resurrection
               and descent, emergent massive
               coiling heads, set beneath all that stone
     here, a grinning sot, there a scarified warrior,
     who spreads his fronds like threading wings, one birthed
     of this trimmed whisperer lush among the grapes—
     and out of his mouth, the vines begin—word
          or forest—the gate to the world—
               for centuries lodged in the niches
                    the joints and cornices
                    from which entanglement is spun:
                    green face carved into gray stone
                    ceaseless as birdsong, sourceless
               as mushroom, silhouetted to the ageless rite,

let us climb back in	cantilever of wayward
put on your garment	looming branches,
swollen earth—	fierce-born fever
surging resurrection of	of bearded glance,
of the endless birth,	solitary sentry
borrow, conjured Christ	whose eyes say
shame we must now	nothing as they
green man whose	bore into us,
inside the choirs:	across the pool
and song, high	of carved years,
convicted into vine	all their carvers gone
for ears, moments	into the looming
with leaves woven	arches of the world,
what praise do you intend	hidden blessings
how to name:	over doorways,

               seasons we've forgotten

2. Interlude: Nine Innings

"The others throw to be comprehended. He
Throws to be a moment misunderstood"
~Robert Francis, "Pitcher"

— A House for Last Year's Summer

Nine Innings

for Amira Jarmakani, who taught me the game again

1

Mounded ground, the round within the square.
Strands of the stitched and fingered

grain, in binary exchange, the thin
whip-weapon-wand fleshed against the

half-seen sphere. Two torques. Opposed.

*Able to hold them to one hit, the
starter strikes out the clean-up
batter on three sliders.
[0 runs, 1 hit/ v0—h0]*

*And then: reversal. Worn pocket in time.
Eliot's delicate line between appearance*

*and the wish. Stitched moon
come back full. Solid explosion.*

*The story nears: great loss
within nothingness. The once*

*slipped by the now
just under the tag.*

*Third basement takes his eye
off the ball.
[1 run, 1 hit, 1 error/v0—h1]*

2

The day prisms. The treeless park
forested with us, where motors cease—

where the sandy path returns—and ohs
die out on a long arc. All homers

ride downhill, all runs are jointed.
And the trap of the glove closes

on darkness. A dense-star
blooming within desire.

*Deep fly ties it.
[1 run, 2 hits/v1—h1]*

*First pitch slips by. The twentieth
candle snuffed. But the failure here*

*is stark. And revolves. Each angle
exposed and hidden at once. The fisted ray
refracted along
white lines. The glare*

> of a moment's trim-argument
> driven back up the middle.

> > *The starter stumbles;*
> > *they're spraying it to all fields.*
> > *[2 runs, 4 hits /v1—h3]*

3
The settled meet the known,
who evade: comfortable

anonymity which cradles
the ocular. They

cover territory, scoop the sailing spark
just above the oiled

> > *Close call; shoestring catch.*
> > *He flirts with pulling back in it.*
> > *[0 runs, 2 hits /v1—h3]*

and looming conflagration.

> *Branches long echoed*
> *under the stream*
>
> *become at once*
> *the surface. The calm*
>
> *turning, angled, now jaded*
> *expectations—*

> > *The crowd settles in;*
> > *the pitcher too—*
> > *the wildness of before*
> > *now steadied.*
> > *[0 runs, 0 hits /v1—h3]*

> *outer spilling*
> *of the inning. Burst into the mitt.*

4
Shortened knot, jerked back. As in fishing,
a wide cast, the pool gone shallow.

Speculation has grown digits,
then begun to add

> > *A temporary duel: the fans concentrate*
> > *on how he tips his hat.*
> > *[0 runs, 1 hit /v1—h3]*

eternity. Okay, you want a story:
watch how the continents move.

> *Here the dead*
> *extend a line. Flight etches*
>
> *the lateral quandary,*
> *ricochet of first*
>
> *intention. A martyr's blink.*

Swift dance
around a bag. Bag becomes a button

            They're maneuvering, playing
holding in place   *a risky game. Hit & run. The throw*
the expanse.   *right on the money.*
             [0 runs, 1 hit / v1—h3]

5

Progression in units. The two—in balance.
The four—covering ground. The three—widened

to the jester's throne. The far wall as tension. Hawk
setting the boundary for sparrows.

Beyond: constraint. Endlessness in tall weeds
where we hunted a generation of shadows.   *High drives, nothing*
                 to show for it.
               [0 runs, 0 hits / v1—h3]

The oppositional familiar. Mirrored
quartet. One, like a memory,

crosses in tight and the maze
relaxes, changes. There and here   *He's in his groove: change-up*
                and splitter. Takes down
at once discolored. Disharmony   *three in a row.*
where lightness pierces the corner.   *[0 runs, 0 hits / v1—h3]*

6

No looking forward. Its desert
already here. Like a sleuth, he

clutches the ball behind his back
and spices the red seams.

You've seen this before   *Big hacks come up empty.*
clearly (or not). Storm   *Handing it to them and*
               taking it away. Then
warning where the air   *he leaves one hanging.*
meets the air.   *[1 run, 1 hit/ v2—h3]*
    Rumors are weighted, dangled
    in a beaker; then splintered—

      tranced back to first. Nothing is left
      of the original suspicion. Only reprisal—

> below, a red crystal.
> Sun queried

A chink in the armor; he holds him on.
Distracted, loses his touch.
[2 runs, 2 hits/v2—h5]

> into the predictable
> over the left field wall.

7

Press the cost
against the idol,

the spoken loss
in carnival valleys.

Negotiations settle
half under the ground.

Pinch hitter; a double switch.
In a slump, he comes up
empty again.
[0 runs, 1 hit/v2—h5]

> Fable rises. Heads once more
> address the sky. Pierced, the deck
>
> tilts and all the fury
> spans to right it back,
>
> sail it into
> these hourless hours.

Slowing the pace; he shakes off
the sign. Gives up two liners to
the opposite field.
[0 runs, 2 hits/v2—h5]

8

Tuned circumference,
a circled ground.

The thief shirks
visibility. Two on,
the wheel sprung.
The constant

Visitors threaten; a double
steal. Bring in the closer
an inning early.
[2 runs, 4 hits/ v4—h5]

reveal rust. The patient
know more.

> Variance sweeps its notes out
> like a wavery hand of cards. Desire
>
> cannot touch its object, must choose
> a role, web inches to its reach.
>
> One rapid-spume
> approximating what has just turned.

He's painting the corners;
experience against power.
[0 runs, one hit/ v4—h5]

9

Aftermath. Or resurrection. The final number ready
to duck its head and roll. We step aside

for an empty radiance, dive with pity
toward speculative hands.

Face as a malleable
shivering destiny,

its favors arising
as they disappear.

Play the spoiler; load them up.
All they manage is a sacrifice.
[1 run, 3 hits /v5—h5]

Batter as funnel. Feet pressed out
to form a continent, hands

against the shaven and spun
wound. Married to distance—

something comes close and veils
its lonely tumbling form. Evening

enters. Wings' wide flourish,
speckled and bold.

Here the outcome sequesters
all you've long known:

this race is only
about coming home.

Full count; he fouls it off.
Then one is left over the heart
of forever.
[1 run, 1 hit/ v5—h6]

3. Spiral Jetty

"but if you look long enough,
eventually
you will be able to see me"
　　　　　　~Margaret Atwood, "This is a Photograph of Me"

Snail Along the Allegheny Trail

    Steep descent into this ghostly town
      where the ghostly limbs of Pennsylvania Oil
          and Quaker State refineries still scar
      the flats along the river bend : in Emlenton, ferns
            grow twenty feet from the Allegheny Trail
      and the fence warning visitors away
    from its lost industrial glory. Now winter runners
      jog where stacks burst slag, a tiny stem

    roots in a coagulated chunk of char, a snail
      stretches out its translucent neck
          to cross the asphalt. It's Thanksgiving
      and I am on my way along Route 80
            to eat the feast of hospital potatoes
      with my sister and her daughter
    and her husband of a year. Two tumors
      have been excised from her brain. She cannot place

    the two of clubs upon the ace, nor sense nor see
      the wall before her stumbling steps
          but we will toast this day

      and whatever days emerge from her
              long tunnel. Underneath the ground I know,
      through most of Pennsylvania, crews are blasting
massive streams of hydrochloric acid,
      diesel fuel and any other blend

of chemicals and blind ego they can find
    to stir a last hurrah from the Marcellus shale
        you rest upon, dear Emlenton,
      and that my sister sleeps upon.
            I'll sing her "Simple Gifts,"
          that Shaker hymn, and we'll imagine a valley of delight.
For now, the sun breaks through
    a heart-shaped bole in an oak high on the riverbank,

crews from Texas, Oklahoma, crowd the holiday
    motels along the turnpike, and all the streams
        that feed the Susquehanna, Black Fork and your cold
      gray river spinning its slow circles round this bend
           await the taste of brine. I kneel
        in the leaves, the snail curls to my touch, the runners,
circling back, thud the trail with their hulking sound,
    the chunk of slag in my winter pocket thrusts up a small green hand.

"Where does the dark go when the dark goes down?"

Noël asked, the first evening of spring
warm enough to sit outside.
She was three, splay-haired, a typical

jabbermouth, the glow of unseen stars waiting
two million light years in Andromeda
chained behind the pines. Who knew

what ogres she had conjured in her first
one thousand nights? On the plane from Guatemala
—and even now, at times—she would clench

her body tight and scream like some bright banshee
and only the cage of our arms
around her body could ease her back.

I suppose she may have meant
the human dark, all those sold
across mountain passes, tethered for generations

to the mines, stockpiled weapons, the night raids,
or else that other dark, between the thighs
where eventually all the centuries emerge.

I didn't have an answer. The mauve sky
melted its thick doors. I suppose
all I should have said was, "Here."

Self-Portrait with Drowning

Someone has conjured "shadow of a heart"
   with magnetic tiles over my metallic office doorframe,
and I begin to wonder if this is just borrowed imagery
     or some kind of subtle critique. Have I lived

more like wandering cloth within my days, like a moth
   quivering in the apple orchard, half-
aware of time or flight or the falling red shadows
     all around me, as of the shiver of August

and the invisible hurtling of the globe? Who has carried me
   strings for music as on a shapely wooden dinner plate,
or a mat for kneeling, the stuffed wizard
     and his companion chime? I walk the prairie

without someone to show me where to look and what
   is it I feel? Goldfinches, monarchs
weave in and out of the coriander, jewelweed, but the names,
     the colors slip away from me like notes

I never learned to read. Once I drowned
   at the edge of a continent—three times—
unable to ride the pattern of the waves, to leap
     in unison with their dips and rises. Christian

from far off on the Strait of Magellan, lingered
   on the beach, while his wife and sons made it a game,
laughing on the uprise and keeping their breath alive
     upon their fall. Me, I reversed it, losing

my air as the wave took me down and quietly laughing
   as I struggled below, the saltwater surging
through me and bringing me—sheer luck—
     to shore. Never had the world been so clear,

as if I had been washed clean, as if from that moment
   —it took three visitations—I could live in any tide.

Within One Burning Star
> —afternoon at the Polaris Mall, outside of
> Columbus, Ohio

The woman in her white burka
turns her head quickly my way, as if she had just escaped,
slipping past the swollen heads who guard the eastern door.
Maybe she's not sure if I am some sort of guard myself,
armed with pen and open book, watching her move.
It's hard to listen to myself in here, with the music
slashing its knife under my feet as in some fiery children's game.
It's hard to watch her, or even remember her glance, her quiet
passage through the sea of us. When was she taught
humility? Long ago maybe her face was hidden

in her scarf of white against some desert's or some suburb's
sands. And she finds her way now, one more shadow
through the shiny stone mirrors. All the models
on the posters look like wary strangers. Frame your head
they say: see, we have no eyes so what is left of you? Who
gave you breasts, legs, bras, jeans? Try on
these gestures, hips tucked, thin plastic necks
poised, forever screwed into these smudged
white shoulders. Everywhere, I take a clock— it sits
before me now. What sliced arm of time, what ambulance

down some southwestern roads could be heard
this far away? I am at last a spangled band, skin tuned
into light, like darkened fireworks falling over Ohio fields.
I am a pea coat from the night sailor, or the man from an alley
who lifted it off your shoulders. I know what they want, that never
in the next 100 years will I turn around. There may be hordes there,
a siege of armies, beheadings, a flood. The love of my life
could appear out of woods and come running. Like Lot's wife,
like Orpheus leading his buried heart out of the ground, like Odysseus
tied to the stake of his mast lest he leap into the sirens' surf,

they hope I will never, never, never turn around.

— A House for Last Year's Summer

For Zita

Dusk-dawn. Lithuania. The vested autumn mornings
when her mother led her to the forest mushrooms—

those white and sculpted sails, underground streams of delicate
decay. Years later, in Chicago, she could still recall

the raven-feathered trees, the stories that broke through
her sleep, the curses that wrinkled inside of smiles

at the edge of the roads. Devils appeared, courting
the village maidens, who tricked them

by stepping on their toeless shoes, unbuttoning their tails
in the center of the dance floor. Always there are crowds

that open up her canvasses, still asleep
and naked in their wanderings through clouds

and shoreless doorways. Soldiers in camps
whose numbers bleed onto their shoulders,

her brother who rises, months after he disappeared,
amongst a thousand languid bodies, like a sound

out of the sea. Homes vanish. Her mother like a shorn saint
slips into a veil. Her brushes dipped into hand-crushed walnut

wrap the Wall around the gallery. Here now, close the doors
upon the ones within, who never saw it coming,

who never knew their sorcerer's name, whose maps
have melted, whose sand has found the single eye,

whose names will be splintered by an arrow. This mirror
tips inside a pool. The kitchen floor

lays checkered with age, the players having passed through
into the sliding time. Faceless in robes spun

out of the ochre mountains, they enter onto plains that will recede
forever toward the edges of the moon.

and only one pass through—dear soul—
whoever, on this day, the legends pluck awake.

Terry Hermsen —

Variations

    1/ Brueghel the Elder
He held the knife
to the center of the fish

but all that came out
was the blindness of the feast.

    2/ Holsthorst
The precision of the paint
is matched by his attention to the small.

How carefully Delilah watches her scissors
make the first slice into Samson's hair.

    3/ Magritte
I know a moon—she nightly dreams above me.

    4/ Magritte
Through the window, we are all reversed.

    5/ Hopper
No—nothing (not even the forest
or the red late-summer grass

or the man polishing again
the glass of the pumps) is lonely here.

    6/ O'Keeffe
No mourning.
Her desert road

calls the stars aloud.

    7/ Smithson
He crawled inside his spiral
at the edge of the Great Salt Lake.

who was it said the waters
wouldn't rise?

— A House for Last Year's Summer

To C.Y. Woo (1898-1989)
                for the Frank Museum (Westerville, Ohio)

On a light winter day, the windows
shape the gallery

till we walk the rooms unable to tell
our footsteps from shadows.

These swaths of light
invade the frames as well:

rivers crash down
mountainsides, two squirrels
lean close to see me

from bare branches.

One rooster
(thick-black draping tail)

balances on the knotted
blooming branch—

see how gracious—

half the space below him
holds nothing at all.

The Peaches Are Rotting in My Neighbor's Yard

The peaches are rotting in my neighbor's yard,
Their burnished yellow beauty deepening
Every day unnoticed, as if a sun has drowned

Into her trees, the syrup of their darkened
Skin grown bruised, her daughter sunning as
The peaches are rotting in my neighbor's yard.

Finches along the edge voice their alarms
And her foil gleams, her beauty slipping
Every day, unnoticed, as if a sun has drowned

And she must patch it up with some mellifluous tar
To fold within an earth she finds too searing.
The peaches are rotting in my neighbor's yard.

What mottled, silent solace can compare
With all that speaks so loud within our hearing?
Every day, unnoticed, another sun is drowned,

And I, behind the fence, can't stop it going down
Nor raise the volume of its muted warning.
The peaches are rotting in my neighbor's yard,
Every day unnoticed, as if a sun has drowned.

She Lives Above the Bakery
for Joanna

Cloud cover. The always-sweatered mother
and her son, who pick up every Thursday
their two sacks of day-old rolls, at 9:15, the gravel
crackling to their steps along the alley,
comfort her. She lives alone. Smokes out on the fire escape,
counts——another comfort——the single row
of mismatched bricks, like a childhood's
tilted and long-cracked abacas.

The one backward-swung and dipping branch
of the awkward maple that frames her sill
makes a portal or a cup of some baptismal fount.
She's tired of school, of standing so far from the world
she cannot knead its skin,
of filling up with eyes and words
like bubbles dancing in the dough.
She wants children——to plant some eyes herself

and watch them grow. No more Shakespeare.
No more charts to claim pretense. She wants
a field, a wedding ring, a hinge in a gate
to open like a lauded, ribboned hand. A staggered order
to keep a balance, like that river-line of mortar
in the patched and lovely old warehouse wall
that angles out away from plumb
and lets the rain drip down.

RiddleWish

This must begin elsewhere, like a breeze
in high branches of which the tree itself
is unaware. But what is the tree?
And what are you? A sturdy consciousness?
A focus on maintaining roles? You
tilt, slightly, and wait (studiously, unconsciously)
for a mirror move. Maybe the fulcrums
that balance the planet need a slight
adjustment and you are the only one
who can measure the delicate, wordless
quivering. Raise your cupped hand—this
is almost speech—testing the corresponding
sway. You may have to lift a lithe, threaded
veil, woven or free, stained by sunsets
or the inner glow of wood. And here you may
pause—there seems to be no rush—
though words are forming beyond dictionaries
or a steady lexicon. Maybe they can only
be read without a frame, or so close
they disappear, the page you focus on
reading you back, following the story
you thought was yours alone, now drinking
from the bowl that swallows you,

both hands raised to make sure.

— A House for Last Year's Summer

The Floating World

And so I returned to your stale yellow row of apartments
    by the railroad tracks, every unit the same
  yet together intricate as a beehive. Is it the body then

which pulls us in, and not history or radiance
    or memory? The grass spread out, dry as hay,
  and the trains roared through full speed

like rumblings of far-off war. So many nights
    we'd barely make it halfway through a movie
  before we'd end up on your floor

and you'd ride above me as if we too
    were some sort of train, your long legs
  so easily rising up and down in ecstasy

and I'd lift into your nakedness so fiercely
    I'd have to force myself to watch—everything
  moving so much it was like we'd pressed our skin

into the walls. Little boxes of hundreds of us
    in our yellow hexagonal combs all after
  the same infusion. One midnight

you took me down to the pool, empty
    and closed, though the gate still opened,
  and in your tight-ribbed suit held me to your waist

and bid me lean back, my legs wrapped
    around you, as if I were a centaur
  and grew out of your belly.

Did I have a soul at that moment?
    I floated as if completely merged into the water,
  that strangely magnetic water,

its artificial blue my final
    and quite temporary bed. The night
  fell back into its honey and my hold on you, once again,

was not enough. Cold moons like jesters
    puppet the years
  and we do our best to glide within their dance

Terry Hermsen —

till they shut down, slowly, and lay us back
    onto a river, longer than any blue current
  we could conjure, and we shiver then—without souls—

and disappear again into the floating world.

— *A House for Last Year's Summer*

Spiral Jetty/Mirror Span: Homage to Robert Smithson

*"Pictures of the future slip from my sight
through the progression of mirrors."*

i/

From the beginning perhaps he plotted not his death
but his disappearance. Not the biplane collapsing

into one of his own earthworks, but a sudden leap (age 22)
 where only machines
made the art, with all its white and sculpted lines,

narrowing cubic arcs. Genius New Jersey boy
who took the train into the Village

now structures structures where the human body
does not exist.
Now shovels angle rock salt

—mirrored corners of a gallery—
wall and floor and wall—and NOTICE: his art speaks to his art

in sharpened shadows of a broken jewel.

ii/

Sight site	Slight spite
Rough rock	Art shock
Buried building	Half exposed
'Dozer opens	Earthly wound
Pour glue	Down a slope
Photograph it	(Massive joke)
Self-fueled viewers	On a walk
Parading panels	Send them back
To where they're standing	Site turned in
Sight turned outward	Crusted skin

iii/

He:
Ribs red steel construction flats into
 four-foot slatted box.

Pours rough large quarried rocks till their gray jagged edges
      push against their prison.

Is (perhaps) inside, shoved against the confines,
      all presence/jagged release.

He: as real bird
cageless—in this real room.

iv/

```
                        buried below
            peninsula          our eyes
          swirled              order of the galaxy
           distant             shudders in the brine
                               he walks in a spiral
                               where his mind once
                                scaled to rock
                trembling      hardened
   braided insurrection  spinning   homespun resonance
 bulldozed desert curse      birth      buried backward clock
   August intervention               camera
   slowly disappear                  holds the archer
      their own lake                 close within his bow
       then beneath                  ardent adolescent
    their looming pier               fierce to let it go
   listen to the days shake          pearls of the target
        congealed into cold          shine in thickened stone
                radiant star enactment
```

v/

    In the end   perhaps it is
    his own body   that spans
    everything   together

    as if he were   a mirror himself
    far above the day   & floating skyward

    near-thinness   of air
    where he lies   pulls out

    kicks—steadied   by one edge to the
    ragged   glacial face

— A House for Last Year's Summer

    & by   the other
    to his   childhood

    these split   New Jersey outcrops
    rockcreeping   ten feet
    apart   per century

    as if the rock   were dripped
    in slowing motion   from the clouds

    & we   glance up
    toward   nothing,
    or down   where

    light sets its   shadow-minnows
    swimming—that grand   non-space
    any moment that   surrounds us—or no
    as he always said,   swallows.

Terry Hermsen —

Lament for the Dead from an Island in the Rain
Two deaths, Atlantic City, July 7th, 2015

It's raining on the island where these words find mooring
And two men are dead along another coast.
The waves pour in and, yes, the water's rising,
And both faces face another darkened cloth.

What is the lament when knives are so ready?
The dead will walk those streets for months to come.
A man leans on a fence, a boy bends his head in,
Neighbors gather but cannot return home.

Within the rain I hear the shots and sirens.
Redwing blackbirds squawk among the reeds.
7th of July, but no one else is singing.

Someone's fallen. Someone's son. The mad one turns
To stab a second time—and runs—the rain increases,
The bullets burrow, we are all less. Again.

On the Gift of Three Artificial Candles

In the box, three candles, the batteries slid
Inside. Plastic, with a plastic sheen, but hazy
As a certain kind of wax, wrapped round the bulb,
Hidden as the flame of sex, unreachable
And so alone. As when we're in the room, the mirror
Darkening your shape, so lovely I can hardly look into
Your darkened eyes. But what is risked with these—
No danger of burning down the house, the match

Struck out, its broken tongue seeking
Another spark. Oh turn them off, love,
Bring your light, smoldering below the skin,
Your pupils widening full to take me in,
Stand shell-less, ask, who are we now—
Tremble where the grit strikes, the fire grows.

Terry Hermsen —

Wrinkle in the Carpet
Henry Ossawa Tanner, "The Annunciation"

Waves of sleep and waking
break over fields of time
to this floor where we sit,
nearly prostrate before Ossawa Tanner's

Annunciation, with its column
of swirling light to stand for
the Angel. Thirty years ago
we ate dinner with our legs dangling

over the concrete drainage pipe,
the dark stains of limestone
draping our little valley,
and it felt no less of a ceremony.

Marriages, births, other cities since,
spark their calls, proffer obligation,
stumble toward these robed
unsayable words: the red-orange blanket

hung as an impromptu bedroom
for the young Arab girl
awakened just now, flames
on either side of her, vessels

the same, and her face aghast
with longing that this should be
her promise, her bare toes on the carpet
saying yes, saying no, saying yes.

Noël Escapes

Remember, the stairs still have voices
and the door is the night's ovation.
Each wall pretends solidity behind its flowered sheen

then drinks just as easily from the moon's scalded
long-lipped ewer. Thirteen trees
surround the house and a hundred birds

sleep according to a winged book's
catechism. It's been so long since holy
was a word she even thought of

or walked out on a line of light
pretending to be a vapor. So loudly
do we fit into our uniforms.

The corn dries from its roots
upward. The rivers that burst bridges
and crush through roads are far away.

Here are the bells she must snip
to meet the night. Each one shimmers once
in her hand, then swings on only silence.

Terry Hermsen —

When the Musician Moves Into His House

When the musician moves into his house
he nicks the corners, scaling the past.

Most of the shadows compacted around the edges
grow lazy, for a while, listening for cues.

He will travel miles, trading in flutes, studying
the master whistler, avoiding the hangers of words.

There are plants called epiphytes that grow
only on air, rest so lightly on the branches of their hosts.

There are prairie coneflowers whose small egg-shaped heads
only darken with seeds in the late turns of August.

But now it is time, school is over, the drums
have drawn the children out the long, twisting hallways.

At the edge of the baseball field, a fox enters
from the scattered woods, as if a song always plays

along the chalklines, alive and invisible
and parading in the moments no one sees.

That's where he'll live, and it will be a wayward temple,
the goldfinches plucking the spiraled seeds of the sky.

— A House for Last Year's Summer

Goldfinches with Meadow

for Susie—in remission

<pre>
              Goldfinches weave
      the living heights   in and out of pines
      the oaks that name   and us—call us
     the pines, the aspen,   to our perch above
         winds to stir   the meadow, teach us
       bring us a dozen   the questions
       or imitate union,   of sleep and days,
        midair, mid-July   the random play of
      and detection. Mate   cards and discontent,
    for moments from flight   cures and illusion.
        like them, hidden   They undulate,
             yellow leaves   land in a tree
                  with scattered
</pre>

4. Interlude: Las Botellas de la Eternidad

"Wherever they went, they raised the land ... But words fell like pebbles out of the boots of the barbarians, out of their beards, their helmets, their horseshoes, luminous words that were left glittering here ... our language. We came up losers ... we came up winners ... They carried off the gold and left us the gold ... They carried off everything and left us everything ... They left us the words."
~Pablo Neruda, *"The Word"*

Las Botellas de la Eternidad: A Sequence for Chile
a Daniela y Pedro… y Guillermo

1.

First afternoon in Santiago, I'm trying to read
      the light as the early light of spring.
  The branches outside my temporary home

have years of practice at listening, or perhaps like me
      they nod their heads well,
  not taking in a word.
                Languages dance like goods lain out on thin
  blankets along Provedencia, though I have never
read poems by candlelight
     in the heights of the open cathedrals of the Andes,
or inside the buried observatory at Atacama,
      the catacombs of the blindered
  astronomers.

One square *cuadra* from here, the courtyard
    of one house is locked up and condemned.
Books are being removed behind huge orange swaying cloths

  and sold to caravans.
         Along the metro ride, from Pedro de Valdivia
  to Baquedano, a white balloon slips quietly
up and down the length of the car,

   pausing now at one person's feet,
then another's, anointing us
    from below. A little wind through the open window

  enters from the white mountains.
It has come a long way to look for its wandering child.

2.

The stage is nearly dark. The bass player comes out
    dressed in black
  and stands before a bowl of water
       set on a tall glass stand and lit

from below. And now he begins
     to play the water with his hands,
               drops falling from his fingers,
      notes rising from their settled transparency.

Water is heavy, is us,
    it does not know nations. A ship

full of water would sink through the water and never
reach port, so desperately does it want to join what
    is not named.
                    My friend sinks
    his whole hand into a new measure.
And I remember *mi viaje*,
        the plane that will
    carry me like a womb above
                            the thick and earthly air.

3.

In the museum of eternity from the spine of the Andes
las botellas hacen chistes, their spouts so thin
like little chimneys, their tiny caverns hidden

                    below faces and creatures
    who behind the glass
grasp the spotlights' studied flavors.

You can hear the slosh of waters
within, the running of Tolitan, Chorrazan,
    or Chavinian streams.
                        Two rowers sit, surprised,
  above their little boat, the waters pouring
through and around them.
    Long they have crossed the sierras
    between jungle and coast, exchanging gods

with the shifting colors of the sun.

And, stretched on her stomach
   atop her wide bowl, her legs lithely forming
its lip, a one-day-dreaming child rests

      her chin upon her folded, fluent arms
to look down
   over the deep and terraced valleys.

I wander between centuries. A ten-year-old girl with a portrait
   of Marilyn Monroe on her chest,
      as if her black t-shirt were a living movie

screen, flits around her mother shifting
   from case to case. Still a moment, they pause
  with me before the bottle of a cat,
its bronze worn nearly gold with use,
    its elongated belly feeding
its six-kitten brood, each small

— A House for Last Year's Summer

as half a finger,
    who tipple, like us,
at whatever they can find
  with their hungry, nuzzling tongues.

                 4.
Sunday morning in the side garden of the Hostal Chiloe,
      on the street of Bernando O'Higgins,
  three lilies have opened
their effusive and brilliant white collars
    while two more stand like tapers ready
        to unfurl their scrolls of green fire. Like you,

my love, no one would see these from *la calle,*
    pressed as they are between the broken
  sidewalk and the enclosing scraggle

of bushes, except maybe the sky.

      Last night I talked philosophy with my traveling companion,
Guillermo,
    a teacher from the Thomas Jefferson School in Concepcion,
            and a former manager in the Chilean forest industry.

  Now he shows students the making of telescopes
      or how to construct bridges of tiny sticks delicate
    and nearly strong enough
to reach *Araucania.*
                Between us we know a child's language
    but John Dewey and chaos theory

and the fractals of the body and the sea,
and the monocultures of eucalyptus and Monterey pines
    feeding the world's paper tongues swirled around our table

 in the empty upstairs restaurant
playing syrupy renditions
    of twangy Beatles' songs.

I am on the other side of *down,* my dear,
    nearly to the glowing southern pole, and ready to reverse,
  falling *up,* riding the tail of El Sur

to bring it home to you,
    where the houses tumble inside
  an unpasteurized green,
      where a wooden Christ stares down

the long Pan-American highway before
acres and acres of wavering eucalyptus
   which draw the water off the deep
                        tables below.

       The children hide
   in their chaotic playground at the Thomas Jefferson School
       to pop out from behind concrete columns,

   where one timber industry physicist
turned teacher builds with them webby silver
     scales to measure the wavering light
                    of Jupiter and the churning
          volcanoes of Io.

5.
Watch your steps up this platform, its wood turned gray
    as weathered bones and some of its skeleton missing,

  three-tiered and bent into its hillside like some old monastery
for ascetic monks. You climb its 30 steps to look

    both ways toward the sea. If there are spirits here,
  they have taken the form of bees that hum within

the hedges—and the orange-throated Chucao,
   half-hidden in the splintered sun.

Farmers' work surrounds you—that of the Swiss-trim fields
     and that of the salmon-pens out in the bay.

   In one, *las ovejas y vacas* wander with the same languages
they use in the Alps. In the other, not so.

    The schools that were once swift and gray within
  the waves spawn now in the smallest of cages.

(Soon they will find a way to flay them
   even as they are born.)

It is a strange religion that dictates your pilgrimage now,
    a shrine on the way from Castro

   to Achao, where the *golondrina* dip

across the fields like white-throated

   cousins of the light. Someday you will put on
a tiny gray coat like theirs and your god

will be the insects you feed into your dance.

All Monday the skies hang low, La Gran Isla
   moving under them. Which way on the planet

 is "down"? The waters do not stay still
long enough to tell us. An old man hauls

   a wheelbarrow along Ruta Cinco, which crosses
the channel at Puerto Montt. No one can keep the thick false-

yellow espinuco from crowding out the native
   blooms nor the highway ads from selling

 ineradicable poses.

At lunch you stop in Ancud to sit
   below a poster of the ancestors of Chiloe,
by Alejandro Battiendos, entitled *"De Presencias
y Ausencias"* and wonder

   if we all are.
      So many names are scrawled
across the walls of nearly every Chilean town,

even on the white alcove of *Nuestra Senora de los Dolores*,
   the beautiful wooden cathedral of Dalcahue.

Your days collapse into tri-fold maps
   and you'll forget, no doubt, even the grand hotel

 at El Lago de Todos Los Santos with its black beaches
ground down from the lava. Even the moment

   when the sky cleared high over Petrohue,
after a full day of clouds and rain,

there at the base of the Andes,
   even the tail of the 86-year-returning comet,

 one spark of which offered you
   a meteor to ride across the sky.

6.
When I left my body it fell back
>   like a large heavy doll. And whoever I was
> kept trying to prop me back up

>   as I slid halfway in, halfway out
>   of myself. Below,
>   the traffic of Santiago still churned

the night air. And the bodies of the dead
>   from the coasts and islands up
> and down the hemisphere brought me

>   their centuries like small cups of dark wine.
In the sculpture park across the Río Mapocho, channeled as it is
>   into its flowing tomb, an angel of wire

mesh and concrete wings enters *su vuelo primero* daily
only to be caught—daily—in the knot of her own robes.
>   She is headless.
>   In the National Ballet's staging of Verdi's "Requiem,"
>   all was white and red and black and the dancer
>   on the huge last-supper-length table

>   made of it such a solitary stage.
Perhaps she was Christ again, drowning in the splay
>   of each body lost, stroking as best as she could

every edge of its expanse
>   as it lifted and tilted and in the end
> became a wall.

7.
Speechless all day I read poems, expecting little, answering only
>   to the faces painted beside the doors, planning nothing

 now, simply arranging
for the three-tiered eyes
>   of the buses to open on time,

 for the old man across the alley

to pulley his shirts out
>   to dry from his fourth-story window,
> for the jugglers to leap

 as the traffic stops,

— *A House for Last Year's Summer*

      this guitarist and piper to choose
   the bench beside me, starting

and emptying their songs
   with such precision, as if they were lowering buckets
into a well.
               The houses here open all their beauty
   inward, setting up illusions where the locks
  clink inside us, as if the women
could disappear
into rivers, and the men mottle themselves
   into the courtyard sycamores.
                      Like them, I travel
in multiplying zeroes, sentences that do not
   erase themselves.

Pedro tells me of *el buitre—the vulture—*
     which we either see or not.
"No in-between," he says and lifts his eyes.

It settles beside us
   in the sudden forests, or here
 in the mirrored mountains
where the skyscrapers square off

   their disguise. At every moment consuming death
or if we do not see, consuming *us*.

Under the archways to the museum, so many
   of its treasures scraped up from
                      the floors of caves,
   the fortune tellers sit
at tiny folding tables.
  The days implode with an almost-language,

like Pedro's "best picture," which he saw
   but had no camera for—the dark house of the poet
 by rocks of the sea

completely wrapped in black plastic swaths.

    Friends return from twenty years abroad.
Restaurants open onto fountains. At the corner
   of Providencia y Los Leones a mime painted all copper

holds a frozen miner's pickaxe
   until someone drops him coins.
  Glossy models span the metro walls

and the upper windows of *las tiendas*, all arrogant
    as the stone profiles
  of the Inca's (or the Spanish) henchmen collecting tithes.

Tonight, near midnight, I will leave
    the dark mirrors of Chile, where no one watches
   the mountains from the trains of Santiago but where everyone
knows they are there.
          The crowds will keep passing
   as on the streets of any city

and I will disappear, as if a fantasy
    could be walked through, as if the best words
   were the ones that were never said,
as if I too were painted with the colors

  of the invisible mines.

Phrases in Spanish (by section) 1/ Cuadra = city block 2/ Mi viaje = my journey 3/ Las botellas hacen chistes = the bottles make jokes 4/ La calle = the street 4/ Araucania = one name for the southernmost areas of Chile 4/ El Sur = the South 5/ Las ovejas y vacas = sheep and cows 5/ Golondrina = swallows 5/ Nuestra Senora de los Dolores = Our Lady of Sorrows 5/ "De Presencias y Ausencias" = "Presences and Absences" 5/ El Lago de Todos Los Santos = The Lake of All the Saints 7/ Espinoca = a thick-branched, yellow-flowered invasive bush 8/ Su vuelo primero = her first flight 9/ Las tiendas = the stores

5. The Smallest Ripple

". . . like a spell
like signs executed
by the superstitious,
who are the faithful of this world"
 ~Adrienne Rich, "Pieces"

— A House for Last Year's Summer

Palabras Parejas

Los pulmones, the lungs, burning in nodes of stars without names.
Los pulgares, the thumbs, jutting from behind the curtains of the fingers.

La vela, the sail, creased from its long months in drydock.
La vela, the candle, who shows up late for the party, relishing shadow.

La sombra, the shadow, lonely, retrieved from its worn sack.
La sangre, the blood, who so quickly learns to dry.

Las piedras, the stones, that one by one bring the mountain down.
Las piernas, the legs, so shining in the stream.

La cereza, the cherry, the one I picked with darkened lips.
La cerveza, the ale, bubbling burnished ore from the fields.

Hermosa, named beauty, dancer who changes in every light.
Mi hermana, sister, who only signs her name when discovered by surprise.

Los hombros, shoulders, that measure the weight of sun.
Los hombres, the men, like stirring cauldrons of longing.

Mis faltas, long mistakes, screwed down in their telling.
Las faldas, the skirts, that speak with such thin tongues.

La estrella, my star, my little eye, you showed up weeping at the back door.
La escuela, old school, you led me past the channel of quivering days.

El miedo, my fear, I laid out your twisting brick streets too many nights.
La miel, golden honey, feast composed in a tiny lake.

Los huesos, thick bones, harden with the war.
Los huevos, the eggs, conjure their fragile years.

Las palabras, the words, follow their stray masters.
Las paraquas, umbrellas, invite the winking sky.

Age Warps

Age warps like a kind lover, her head
in the hollow of your shoulder. She feels
so good there after her long journey
across the globe. You're here, caving in
along a line of demarcation you immediately
ceded to her touch. She has the eyes of a child.
In them you watch the ship of your face
sail off and skirt the shoals. Foghorns
repeat the same chords as yesterday,
their johnny-two-note melody you begin to hum.

**

Age warps the walls. The dozen steps
up to the porch you deconstruct in segmented
breaths. Who were you at the base, or gazing
out the windows? Daily you lay out the charts
of your confessions, compose your absolutions
in the absence of the judge, the failed
architect. The tape measure? It's spun
back on its loop of darkening numbers, loose measurements
for a cheek bone, an aural canal growing hollow.
Add the separations, concave losses whose arc
of sums forms a clasp, a kiss, another face.

**

Age warps. Refusing descent. Blood in the cup,
tiny scales for the jeweler's eye. We disappear
down lenses, parading pronouns, grasp mostly
the knobs to the same old rooms. But here the blind
are scraping back their sight, the sentences hovering
in corners with their ticker-tape machines. Nots unknot
and wrap your shoulders with all you never learned.
And it is she again. Here beside you.

— A House for Last Year's Summer

Fractal Walk

for Alice Fulton

On the stage, half-constructed for the last production
    blue lines shoot out   to help the actors imagine

the universe. Why am I,   before the carpenters arrive,
the hunter of wisdoms,   counter-sinking into my mind the bolts

of this man-made cliff?   (I'd rather've been on the stage crew.)
    Plumb lines arrange the stars   to seek a way out of silence.

    So much room   when looking out from the stage.
    So narrowed   the eyes of the audience.

Before the staggered stairs   of the apartment house on Plum
    I sit among seeds   of a myriadic maple.

White stucco. Lurid irises   with their folded-over tongues.
You fix your screen door, #10,   with sheets of plastic

    and strips of white tape.   And these must be
your bedroom curtains   with floating smiling skulls.

Clock shop—weights   and faceless hammers—
    pendulums at different   earthly paces

    inside of glassed   half-opened hearts.
When I could barely see,   I thought I could make out

    the seconds moving   on the red quivering
    measuring hand   that was school.

    Surely the hereditary   clock repairman
    waits inside   his grandfather's beard.

He does not   worry too much
about his reflection   in the darkening sundial.

Abandoned Shinto shrine—   is it empty now
    or full of us?   And are there voices

    that are required   for silence
or must we   become blossoms?

Terry Hermsen —

No matter how many times
there's always one
I shake the branch,
that falls too late.

———

Museum
tucked into the neck
of the Underground
of the library.

Traced in blue-print:
down the center
Africa Road
of Ohio.

Three velvet roses
tell how many
at the carriage house window
for dinner tonight.

Twenty years later, a village
given the name
of the freed
of a continent.

In a hundred,
choose this swarm of houses
the bulldozers
to drown for a dam.

No photos in these drawers
When you were buried under
of you, viney graves.
a hundred feet of concrete

no one could look
There were too many
down into your walls.
surging voices

to hear them all
and the names
inside the singing water—
that keep on walking.

Judge and Defend
(a riddle)
for Riccardo

In this crystalled world you must consider sky,
where it suspends, where it sails on, and not only now

but after the wrapped dreamers have spoken, their timed
elegance risen from the dead. These thoughts

may not be rushed but parry the full and stationary
parade at once, as if one could stand in the midst

of beauty and not be distracted by what cannot be claimed
or known. For not a single dancer is the same, much

as each maps its awkward patch of sun, much
as any darkened predilection can only be guessed

as the planet leans in to listen. How cruel. These possible
arms will hold nothing, like wavery intimations

of the coming flames. While these others
arch and preen amongst the crown of their singular

restored splendor, arriving in unison. They too
will have no choice and only your knife, the sharp-

grinned smile of your jawed knife, as much a part of hand
as plan, will shut and make it so.

Sugar Maple

Far from the voices, the tree pulls me up
into its gray evolving spiral. Here nothing need be proved,
only the wide July day, thick with ants,

their homes in the roots, their curious persistent highways
up the trunk. Out in the meadow, pairs of goldfinches, like clipped
and undulating pulsating flames

light on the gritty thin strands of coneflowers, adding
hardly a sway as they pluck the heads clean
like tiny Russian hats, leaving rows

of dark indentations, continuous sentences in braille repeating
all one word. For the finches the heights I've climbed in an hour
would hardly be the thrust of two

incantations. Oh why then not stay
up here? I've walked the loosened melodies, held open
the veil for love, trimmed my face

in the mirrors till it's thin as a fan, melted
the eyes of candles, turned the columns
of the glassy sandstone cities. Here

my arms are long and supple, multiple as some
Midwestern Shiva, my evil columns entwined with their redemptive
silhouettes, no head but this dark stubbly

phylum flowing skyward
and rootward, at least a half of me
webbed below the ground, so heart-hollow

I can feel my limbs 20 feet or more in all directions
ride each small breeze, shift for a furious
and sudden rain, hardly a drop winding its way down

to my ghosted inner ground.
a wildfire could sweep this meadow
and I would still stand, singular and scarred, recording that summer

like a knife in my bark I'd slowly curl
my bulk around. But here, nearly invisible, a doe
edges a few feet from my calm

drip circle, with her twin fawns who nuzzle

— A House for Last Year's Summer

the dark promise between
her thighs. I don't scare her

with my humid, human breath
now as still as hers, now nearly
as eternal.

Terry Hermsen —

The Smallest Ripple

And now the island pauses as, from the boat,
it disappears.

As the sky turns, as the waves lip and swallow.

The light bends, they say, in wren's eye
or Palomar, the shadow of us aching with all
we must deflect.

If I could I would lie deep inside the morning
as if it were a sea.

Each day the smallest ripple.

The traitor's exile is his desert home: garden
on a cliff, ladder for a door.

Dark expanse to train the heart to story.

The eldest stories trouble the edge
where summer borrows back
its liquid calendars.

No end to how the mountains whisper,
blow up a storm four bands of blue.

The man who climbs this day a ladder
folds up his house, all his grief

held together by the winds.

New Washington: A Memory

For a dozen years or more
no one has borrowed
these back streets
for kisses,
        it would seem,

or else why would this moon
trace your long throat
so lovingly. It must know
the cooings there,
        the way your tongue

awakened mine and taught
a slim silver melody. Hurrah
for light, white dresses, for woven
lacey belts
        to be removed,

for chimney swifts that nest in
hollow Amazon trees—and here,
for this white light that makes
the road away
        so lonely.

Terry Hermsen —

Mark Rothko, "Red Maroons" (1962)
Cleveland Museum of Art

```
                        ashen core
                  body down    wide coffin
              lay this            door - how
      bored of boundaries            can I shape
           how can I                   my falling
          grate of sound              division whole
            slumber                    narrow verge
           rainborn                   verse lip tongue
    wordscar storm                     swallow
       umber valence                   flight mortem
            throne                    slipped column
             coupled                 vicious nitches
              open favor            eastern pallor
               jostled stone        loose house
                leaden quarry     fade and turn
                       tomb or chapel
```

Sonnets for a Deaf Son

1.

First morning of the summer, he lies collapsed
In bed, today pushed up against the cool green wall
With his left arm curled over his head
As if he were swimming still. He hears
Nothing now and must be tapped awake, his back
Rubbed, or his head. Or else decide for the light
To call him, wander the scaffold of the stairs
Where so many wars have left the fallen
Sprawled below their failed night assault.
Today it will be an hour or two before he places
His magnetized ear against his skull—
That life-line pulling toward the swarming shore
Of words. This day he'd rather float alone
—At least a while—within the season's swell.

2.

Days of heat collide with June. By afternoon
The hood of sun closed in. He sees the shining beetles
Begin their desecration of the cherry's leaves, their ritualed
Deconstruction, as if they were a crew
From the fiery fount of language. The street too
Cracks, the asphalt patched with tar,
The crunched reptilian faces of the cars
Command their spaces down to separate rooms
Inside each house. And he with tiny models
Scouts his own roads, complete with revving sounds
He borrows from the heated world all around.
And speech? Its blind bursts need hardly trouble
The sanctity of codes that etch a world
He kingdoms, crowned, as pure reception's child.

My Father's Houses

Most of my father's houses were drawn on paper, and he
never lived in them. He would curl them up each evening
or let them lay out on his slanted drafting table

for the moon to decipher. Was it possible we appeared
as stick figures hidden inside the lines
working to earn his confidence, balancing on the blue

graphics like his inherited workers
from the discontent construction crew
who would come to tell us *scram, no one*

*can live in a warehouse or the next extension
of the Oldsmobile plant.* It was a long time before
we learned there were no houses at all

and we had to make our own cubicles on scraps. Come
home now, it's way past midnight. His hands
at last have wound under his chin, they grasp

a little night air or hover around a thorn
some songbird in the crabapple has built its nest behind.
When he hears the morning it will have long awakened,

he will have moved us to an English Tudor on a hill
with its thick and arching beams, we will have plucked
up our lives one more time and pulled the curtains in.

This is how I came to predicate the sun, make music
from drainpipes, lie late in bed finishing the stories
for the light. This is how I learned to follow the daze of flight,

the happenstance of plan, to cling to the wheel
long after sleep should have laid me to the ground,
to hold a candle as he climbs the spiral to his final room.

— A House for Last Year's Summer

The Laboratory of Return
    (a riddle)

Beside your wall-less coffin, you keep the world
frozen into tiny pools, tucked and disarmed

into a soft pocket of regret, as if it could turn away
from the endless flickering filaments

of sin and history. Yet here it is again,
so insect-like before you, ready to crawl

and find a high invisible place to hide,
the most obvious of all. You think: it can hear

nothing, nor will it speak your secrets.
I will just borrow it again for a while, you say,

as I have so many days, with its fine divided souls,
its sheer cliffs to gather rain, or tears. You clasp

nearly nothing, with your paired pincer fingers,
remind yourself to be gentle with

this delicate power you hold. It resists,
of course. Its mantis-legs reluctantly

say goodbye to their loving mummy slumber
but, risen, have designs and will only live

one place. You must not force them
out of their desire—to hold you like little dancers

and make you turn your head
anywhere they want. They think you should

be grateful that they cling so close, making niches
from what was once nakedly you.

Without us, they so boldly claim,
two would never equal one.

Silence of Your Eyes

    Silence outside the window, which is the silence outside the mind.
  Silence before the pool shot, which is the silence of intent.
    Silence listening for the motor, which is the silence of leaving.
Silence of the deaf boy, whom you can drive for hours without a word.
    Silence of the deer beside the highway, for whom he watches like kin.
Silence of the bull snake's jaws, unhinged for the swallowing.
    Silence of men, the long drawn silence of men, which eats the miles.
  Silence of the wandering train, so set upon the rhythm of its travail.
    Silence of the will, which works its way down through the shoulders.
      Silence humming, silence of the steady coo.
    Silence stepping around the sleeping man whose cigarette
      has once more hit the floor.
    Silence of his death, at 53, five huddled daughters at the grave.
  Silent stalking of the whooping crane before the dance begins.
Silence of the man who wishes to erase his ironed words.
    Silence of the night growing dim, the simmering of ginger and garlic.
Silence of the roots, the tangled dark another mirror.
  Silence of the rain, the impact and the echoing pools.
    Silence of the adjective and its suddenly wounded sentence.
Silent stir, silent purr, your head tipping sideways in toward mine.
    Silence of desire, your arms like dancers, naked of sleeves.
  Silence of the coins, the hexagrams of their conjured stories.
      Silence before the voice enters the song, the missing beats
        inside the song.
    Silence inside of any chosen note, and its half-hollow design.
      Silence of the wrinkled page, the heat of the long parade.
    Silence of your eyes, dark fissure I am caught between.

— A House for Last Year's Summer

Beautiful Rain

Come, my dear, let's leave the rowing of chairs
And head this morning into the beautiful rain.

The gingko tree, as well, once thought dead,
Breaks out new shoots for love of the beautiful rain.

What drove the flag-torn Sarmiento past his harbor
But thoughts, out there, of one more beautiful rain?

In a rush he awakens, grafted to the tides, he
Knows how his scars will shine in the beautiful rain.

He begins to love the pauses so much he becomes one,
Like a young cloud adrift, preparing its beautiful rain.

Long ago I folded my cantilevered wings, past dusk,
To bask again in the glow of your beautiful rain.

And you answered, though the voices splintered,
Sifted name after name through the wild, beautiful rain.

I retrieved one—Terry—though limp as a flag
Bled out from long war to the wash of your beautiful rain.

Terry Hermsen —

The Elemental

Poem of voices behind a closed door,
As Frost said, or dry wind in upper branches.

Some deep loneliness even in the mantra light
Of memory, folds in the bark where trunks meet earth.

The Ojibway peeled the white bark of birches
For houses, shoes, canoes, blinds against the snow.

Poem as sail, in the mirror, rough turn upon
The keel, tacking the diagonal, oppositional winds.

And you, the years, the circumstance, tan skirt
Up the stairwell, turreted window my salvaged light

Against the shoals. Flare of vest, avenge of rain,
Symphony through the snowstorm, red dress at the door.

Translation of motors, fissures into earth, the probing
Beak of the sandpiper, brail in the mist.

Summer of storms: all that water, Terry, must have
Somewhere to go. Surge of continents. Touch of this hand.

In Africa, Ohio

In Africa, Ohio, today, a woman walks her dogs—
one black, one tan—along the rockbed creek

of the dam, the earthen mound that thirty years ago
reshaped this horizon. Hikers climb that horizon,

stare out onto the water, scan, predicated compasses,
everything they cannot see. Blue water with no real shore—

a reservoir is not a lake—and all that rush of confluence
waiting at the massive drain below. Oh I know that no one knows

how long the dam will last, I know the edges of the sky
will serrate all these colors, shred the remaining faces

passing up into these clouds. But some days I can float out
holding back the dizzy soils that once bespilled

my mind, taking the unseen (one—two,
one—four—two) steps the dark land ponders.

How can I hold a people, scar a cabin deep into
my hand, place a nail between the thornish

bone, gather up the flies? Harness a plow
to my own shoulders and disappear

toward north, hovering as the buzzards
horde, loving the open currents of this valley

too? Pass history back and forth, as always,
between the dead and the living, between those

who are just beginning to climb, and those
who are already coming down?

Terry Hermsen —

Re-Entering Picasso's "Las Saltimbanques"
(repainted by Wolfe Von Lewkiewicz in the 1980's)

Today I will not rush as I sit before this copy of Picasso's circus family, "Las Saltimbanques," meticulously reimagined onto this Wexner Center wall. And that's the message here, isn't it: let's refuse to rush. Let's not worry about what's original, about the mood of the sky, whether there is wind or no wind, leaves or desert, storm or clarity. Learn to watch, whether your world is inside or out, a carbon of some other or your own. We are again and always poor souls, redeemed or unredeemed. Practicing our faces for the trials before us.

The main thing is: can we make the spirits laugh? Not drag on those we love? Can we pattern our clothes with random diamonds, as the two jesters here? Glance with a renewed wryness, as does the central one, looking straight at us, his wide hat the mockery of a toreador's? He holds no sword above his head. Rather, he is just a part of the circus players as they relax and give us a way to enter time. The old fat man sitting on his crate pats the dog's gentle head.

For unlike us they make peace with *nothing*. The stage a mere vehicle, the assumed audience will pass by or not, and either way will leave them alone. The white horse in the distant pasture will soon meld into the mist. And the youngest girl—my favorite—will look out at no one as she balances on her misshapen globe, teaching us again that rising up on toes and the raising up of hands till they touch the very sky.

— A House for Last Year's Summer

A Farewell for Neruda

On the 40th anniversary of his death in 1973

We follow you, *su gente*, in our little rented car,
a stone for our clock, to dip into the waves.
You are a bit too fast for us, you have a driver now

and a sleek 1950s limousine. You have been giving speeches
in the Senate, though the delivery and the shuffling
of the papers hardly pauses. A few look up

as at some plump duck crossing the stage.
They are used to cartoons. They have tiny speakers
plugged into their ears and only hear their music

pre-recorded. It is strange to go on living, to pass
Hotel Neruda, drink beers with pasted labels
and the reflection of your face inside. Strange to wince

at your line of friends swept out again into the jaws
of the new-fascist sea. Especially when you loved
that sea, its anonymity, its Chilean thighs

and rolled your bulk out to lounge in its tides like a seal
lazy on Valdivia's Calle-calle. You gathered partiers
to your fiestas, dressed up in gangster's furs

or you strapped on aprons to serve them all. We are here,
we wander with plates of hors d'oeuvres, climb the black
volcanic rocks. The troops arrive. Hunt for lost poems

and stinging memoirs. Rip open the pillows
to siphon the dreams. No one can touch a single string
or carry a left-over *cuequa* out the door.

We are not sure now if the rot will ever leave. But sleep,
Neftali, among your many lovers. This window, though split
completely through, still faces the sea. A bobbing form

appearing on the waves. You imagine it from
your settled years, a captain's table,
a writing desk. You will make love, illicit or not,

over and over on the gnarled currents buried
in that wood. Your father, your lost mother,
the sawing, as you said, of the great trees,

the weeping of Federico's tiny violins,
the mute boy's voice disguised among the crickets,
all of your friends around the table, and again,

what else? You lift your sailor's glass.

[Spanish words:"su gente" = your people
"cuequa" = a Andean folk instrument,
banned during the Pinochet dictatorship]

A House for Last Year's Summer
for my father (1921-2013)
—*architect*—

What if you turned and there was no hour,
the old jailer's vise unfastened from the door,
the ivory orb of the train's eye through the snow

released, the track gone—and the road?
Simply nowhere to *arrive*, the lynx's paws wide
and merely kneading a species-less tundra,

or rather, the dash of the snowshoe hare
already there below its leap. And the poem
did not conclude, or the book,

or the keep-on-singings. The house
you walked into was the one you *heard*, not etched,
these arms when the world melted.

6. Epilogue: Five Days at the End of the World

"Beneath the page you see a ship and a shipwreck.
You are the ship and the shipwreck."
       -Christian Formoso, "Beneath the Blank Page"

— A House for Last Year's Summer

Five Days at the End of the World

for the Strait of Magellan—and Punta Arenas, Chile

The Portal

1

Place the wind on a post and spin it, like those children's games where
you cannot reach the ball passing and gyrating over your head. So here
the world draws in its air, as Christian says, breathing in a wild rotation.
I move slow, a frail letter, like a candle or a sail trying to burn upright
or at least not drown. The wind is blind and I am deaf. I watch the signs
for how to smile, or not, for all the *pasajeros* holding on in the winds to
the wires of the world.

2

Greg blames it all on *los humanidades*, each crowned scholar scrambling
for life in a little hole in that grand tree, holding on with pickaxes and well-
trained teeth. Look at the world on fire down below, the overturned cars,
the tight hearts of twin explosions, the children gunned down with their little
backpacks on. But here we are eating our Greek scrolls, baked with dusk,
here is the thick jam of theory to make palatable the grit of the bones.

3

Rafael is buying bananas today, far off in Santiago, because tomorrow he
will feed the orphans cereal and toast for breakfast and guide them through
their games. He wants me to feel the words of his faith, walking them for
me forward and backwards. Sometimes he falls into them like a welcoming
bed, he says, tracing a cadence that balances him through the deaths. For me,
he is Alyosha, the brother who wants to bring this Ivan close to the fire.
I hold up the words of his book from this far away and try to touch their
scars as they flare down the tunnel.

Hours of Exile

1

Hours of exile : what does the body want? You shrink, dear friend, while the old horses rise around you. Everything you touch as small as words and the cracks in the street grow. The pampas deny habitation. But here the fissured sculpture rises, thrusts its molten hand up from the rock, dark hand that wants us to think *oil* as it breaks from crevices, oil they'll burn to thrust up colliding columns, twist hands, grasp equations of the sun, reflame our faces from the ooze.

2

Habits of exile : even in the Castillo del Diablo, they channel smiling songs. It is a trick, of course. You cannot tell the devils from the kind. That is the burden of exile at the end of the world. There are no tides, no play of time. Plastic trinkets appear on tombs. The girl soldier at 25 has been taken into the arms of El Señor. You wander through ghosts. It is the Day of All the Saints. They paint the houses for the dead again.

3

Rules of exile : you cannot look back. Constructions in the desert brand a future on the sand. All you worked for, no matter how many years, would not be there, even if you could return. When the healers find an island, they unfurl a sail. Flags for signals in the wind. Their king will be an old man who for years has cultured tiny trees. This will be your Eden, a salient backyard. No longer to drown the lamplight from the stars.

On the Day of the Dead

1

The graves are magnets, pulling these families to their miniature ancestral homes. The walled-in yards, the faces behind glass frozen in well-tended gasps and trinkets. Only the tall, rounded, branch-tangled cedars can stand against this wind, out-living the fallen souls who climb into their tombs today, reassured and painted back in. Only some of the houses have become wild and thatched a bed of rosemary over their breasts: little gardens without names or remembrance nor any mourners with crutches and braces, linking arms.

2

On the Day of the Dead, the eyes of Magellan wake on his pedestal beside his expansive Strait. They are still aghast at their bright and frightening luck, that this channel may lead to glory. How many villages across the Pacific would he have to burn to show the power of Christ, armor, swords and cannons to impress the recalcitrant kings? Can he see his own death, three months away from his bronze visage, the 500 years it will take to spread the local wars around the world?

3

And why have I come all this way from my own dead to honor faces I have never seen? I trail the military band, the pride of Los Bomberos. By evening the secondary city outside the walls continues on. The festive tents, mechanical monkeys, sausages, balloons. And here, the seller of daffodils, which Luis loves because of Shelley's poem, which by next winter will sink into their graves, will wait for the crush of swirling, invasive winds, at the end of the world, to open their hearts.

In the Land of Fire

1

Now the graves are empty. From my window I watch them pour into the streets and what can I do but join them. Fallen from the ship-that-is-now-monument, they unfold from their black plastic inside of which they have learned again to breathe. The naked daughters of the Yamana run with me over the cliffs, their breasts swaying below the tides, gathering crabs. I live in caves, Darwin mocks me and brings a frame to measure my illusions. In the Forest of the Winds, I open flags of fire. In the Port of Hunger, I mount a cannon to claim the throat of the seas.

2

Now that the graves are empty, we guide their new souls through the streets. They need canes and crutches at first, but gradually learn to scrawl their names in awkward letters on nearly every empty wall. Only later they will begin to float on winds, seed the clouds, return to their place of birth. They climb into the bells, open dawn with sirens. They stare back at us in our children's hooded faces wandering around the square.

3

And who will I visit here if the world is now filled, Father of the Spiral House borrowed from the snail, Mother of the Seas, Sister Whose Songs Escape Me every day? I am a sail and a candle still, two wheels following the knife edge of the Strait. The Disappeared remain so, but there is no grave that does not hold their names, and no stone anywhere where I must not bow down.

— A House for Last Year's Summer

At the End of the World

1

Burrow below the winds—what else is there to do—the trees like horses tuck in their heads and wait for a respite that never comes. No one swims here—only in the air, or else when they are turned to bronze and then they get their wings.

2

At Seno Onway, los *pinqüinos* gather on the beach at twilight in a little city named exhaustion. The waves turned green and arctic, the world tipping on its post. At some point in the morning they must know the need to dive—ten to fourteen hours, meters below the sea. Now here they shake it off, as if drunken, at one signal form a line and waver inland through the tunneled marsh. I would too. Stay low. Murmur. Glance back at the darkening sun. Tuck my head and follow below.

3

Something at stake, at the end of the world, that draws me here, though I cannot name it. Maybe like the krill I need to find another temperature within, that nether-myth to see us part the greed. In 1535, Guglielmo de Lorno made a diving bell, bottles of air relayed in bubbles with the touch of the diver's hand. The Yamana wore little here, shifted in their canoes, trained long years to dive down to the sea bed, gathering spider crabs. Other winds control the surface. Evil makes the towers, places masks on all the young. Dive, burrow, dream below. There is a healing.

———

[Spanish words (by poem)

1/ Pasajeros = journeyers1/ Los humanidades = the Humanities 2/ Castillo de Diablo = The Devil's Castle 2/ El Señor = Another name for Jesus or God 3/ Los Bomberos = Firemen 4/ Yamana = One of the early peoples in Tierra del Fuego 5/ Los pinqüinos = penguins]

Clues for the riddles:

A Dormant Order (p.17)
    Ø   Post-retirement duty
Temporary Circumference (p.24)
    Ø   A spoken journey
RiddleWish (p.48)
    Ø   Mouthed yearnings
Judge and Defend (p.77)
    Ø   Clip-joint decisions
The Laboratory of Return (p.85)
    Ø   For the needful reader

— A House for Last Year's Summer

Answers for the riddles – not in order, ØPruning an apple tree ØMaking a bed ØPutting on glasses in the morning ØGetting on and riding a bicycle ØLeaning in to kiss someone

Answers for the riddles: A Dormant Order (p.17)ØMaking a bed
Temporary Circumference (p.24) ØGetting on and riding a bicycle
RiddleWish (p.48) ØLeaning in to kiss someone
Judge and Defend (p.77) ØPruning an apple tree
The Laboratory of Return (p.85) ØPutting on glasses in the morning

— *A House for Last Year's Summer*

Terry Hermsen taught in the Writers in the Schools program for the Ohio Arts Council from 1979 – 2003, visiting schools, prisons, senior centers, as well as conducting poetry night hikes in such places as Mohican State Park, George Rogers Clark Park, Cuyahoga Valley National Park, as well as locations in California and Vermont. He now teaches English, Creative Writing and Environmental Literature at Otterbein University in Westerville, Ohio.

He holds an MFA in Poetry from Goddard College and a PhD from Ohio State in Art Education. He has two chapbooks, *36 Spokes: The Bicycle Poems* and *Child Aloft in Ohio Theater*, from Bottom Dog Press and his full-length book, *The River's Daughter*, also published by Bottom Dog, was co-recipient of the Ohio Poet of the Year Award in 2009. His poems have appeared in the following magazines and journals: *Descant, Fourth River, Hiram Review, The Journal, Lake Effect, The Louisville Review, Measure, South Dakota Review, Outerbridge*, among others. His book on teaching poetry, *Poetry of Place*, was published by NCTE in 2009. He has recently co-translated and published Chilean poet Christian Formoso's book *El cementerio más hermoso de Chile*, for which he traveled to Tierra del Fuego to spend five days on the Strait of Magellan. In 2011 and 2012, he was co-director (and grant writer) for a teacher workshop in Cuyahoga Valley National Park called "Reading the Earth: The Language of Nature."

He is a father of three, a grandfather of two, a bicyclist, gardener and viewer of stars.

Bottom Dog Press
Harmony Series Books

— Poetry —
A House for Last Year's Summer by Terry Hermsen, 110 pgs. $16
And Waking: Poems by Kevin Casey, 80 pgs, $16
Both Shoes Off: Poems by Jeanne Bryner, 112 pgs, $16
Abandoned Homeland: Poems by Jeff Gundy, 96 pgs. $16
On the Flyleaf: Poems by Herbert W. Martin, 106 pgs. $16
The Harmonist at Nightfall: Poems of Indiana
by Shari Wagner, 114 pgs. $16
Ariadne & Other Poems by Ingrid Swanberg, 120 pgs. $16
Breathing the West: Great Basin Poems by Liane Ellison Norman,
80 pgs. $16
Echo: Poems by Christina Lovin, 96 pgs. $16

— Fiction —
Cold Air Return: A Novel by Patrick O'Keeffe 390 pgs, $20
American Poet: A Novel by Jeff Vande Zande, 200 pgs. $18
Stolen Child: A Novel by Suzanne Kelly, 338 pgs. $18
The Free Farm: A Novel by Larry Smith 301 pgs. $18
And Your Bird Can Sing: Stories by Robert Miltner, 120 pgs. $17

— Memoir & Biography —
The Thick of Thin: Memoirs of a Working-Class Writer
by Larry Smith, 236 pgs. paperback $18, Cloth $26
Flesh and Stones: Field Notes by Jan Shoemaker, 174 pgs. $18
Waiting to Begin: A Memoir by Patricia O'Donnell, 166 pgs. $18
Daughters of the Grasslands: A Memoir
by Mary Woster Haug, 200 pgs. $18
The Curve of the World: A Memoir by Andy Douglas 254 pgs. $18
The Way-Back Room: Memoir of a Detroit Childhood
by Mary Minock, 216 pgs. $18
Salvatore and Maria: Finding Paradise by Paul L. Gentile
200 pgs. $18
Kenneth Patchen: Rebel Poet in America
by Larry Smith, rev. 2nd Edition, 326 pgs. Cloth $28
Selected Correspondence of Kenneth Patchen
Edited by Allen Frost, Paper $18/ Cloth $28
Awash with Roses: Collected Love Poems of Kenneth Patchen
Eds. Laura Smith and Larry Smith
With biographic introduction by Larry Smith, 200 pgs. $16

Order online at http://smithdocs.net (Free Shipping)

www.ingramcontent.com/pod-product-compliance
Lightning Source LLC
Chambersburg PA
CBHW021018090426
42738CB00007B/812